Meet the Planets

by John McGranaghan
illustrated by Laurie Allen Klein

Welcome to the first ever, *Favorite Planet Competition.* I'm your host, Pluto, coming to you live from the Solar System inside the beautiful Milky Way Galaxy.

These planets have been around for billions of years. They have been viewed through telescopes and visited by spaceships. And tonight, one will be named the favorite planet!

Without further ado . . . let's meet the planets!

Mercury ☿
Venus ♀
Earth ⊕
Mars ♂
Jupiter ♃
Saturn ♄
Uranus ♅
Neptune ♆

They're solid. They're rocky. They're close to the sun. Here come the inner planets.

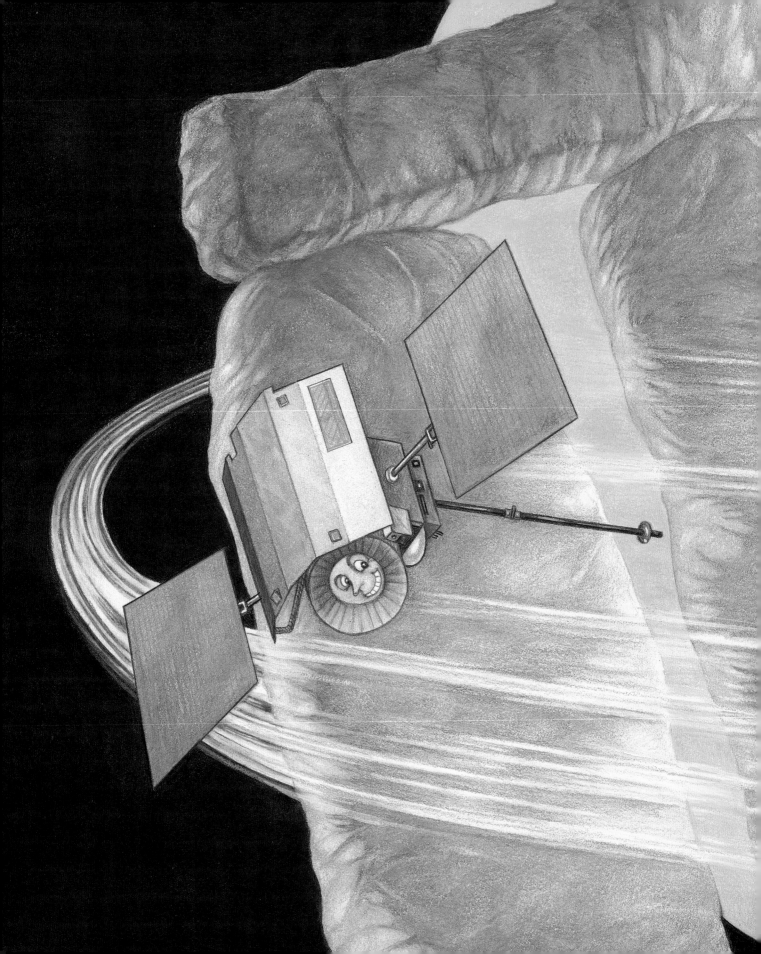

He's a little bigger than Earth's moon and covered in craters; but make no mistake, he's all planet. Circling the sun in just 88 Earth days, he's the fastest moving planet in the Solar System. He's named after the speedy messenger of the gods; now you see him, now you don't . . . meet Mercury!

She's bright, she's beautiful, and she's smoking hot.
Reaching surface temperatures of over 840° Fahrenheit
(450° Celsius), she's hot enough to melt some metals.
As the brightest planet seen from Earth, she's often
mistaken for a star . . . welcome Venus!

Once thought to be the center of the universe by the people who lived on it, she's the third planet from the sun. Not too hot, not too cold, her seas and skies have given life to everything from dinosaurs to daisies. This planet never stops giving . . . meet Mother Earth.

He's slightly bigger than Mercury, but this planet takes a back seat to no one. If he looks a little red-faced, that's because his iron-rich soil gives him a red rusty color. Early astronomers thought he looked like blood and named him after the god of war. Here's the last of the inner planets . . . don't mess with Mars.

They're big. They're far from the sun. They're full of gas and they all have rings. Welcome the outer planets.

He has a red spot the size of two Earths. There's no rocky surface on this planet—he's all gas. But with a surface temperature of -235° Fahrenheit (-150° Celsius), he's not blowing hot air. Named after the king of the gods, he is the largest planet in the Solar System . . . the massive, gassive Jupiter.

Surrounded by a dazzling display of rings, some say he's the most beautiful planet of all. He's the second largest planet in the Solar System, but don't let his size fool you. This planet is so light on his feet that he floats! He is named after the god of agriculture . . . welcome Saturn.

Don't adjust your eyes; this planet is slanted. Since he spins on his side, one of his poles gets 42 years of sunlight, while the other gets 42 years of darkness. This was the first planet to be discovered by a telescope. He was named after Jupiter's grandfather and Saturn's father . . . meet Uranus.

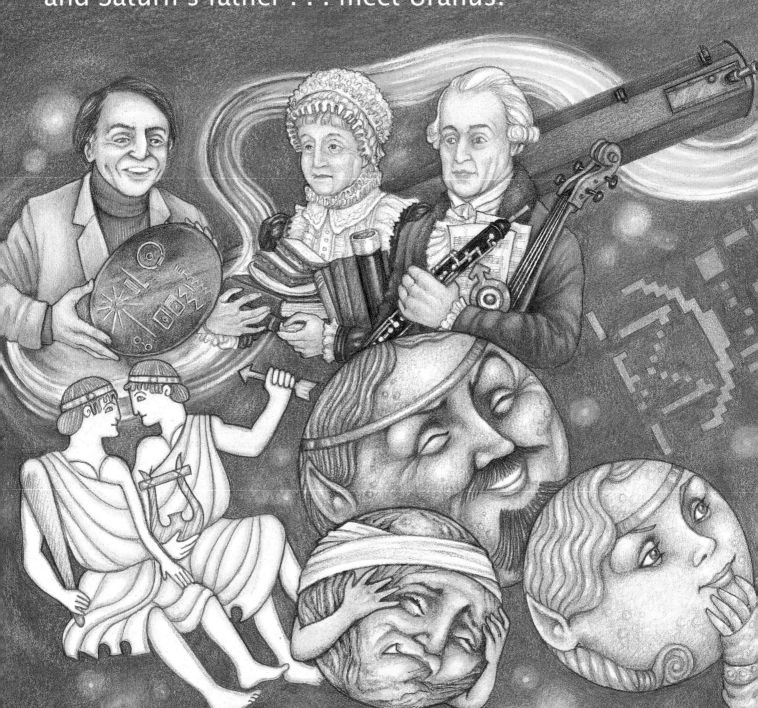

Before telescopes could find this planet, astronomers used math to predict his existence. This beautiful blue planet is anything but calm. With winds swirling over 1,000 miles (1,600 kilometers) per hour, this is one stormy planet. Hold onto your hats . . . here comes Neptune.

There you have them. All eight planets dressed in their Solar System best. Let's have a big round of applause.

Girls and boys, earthlings and aliens, I have just been informed that our judges cannot reach a decision. The moons have declined to vote due to a conflict of interest. The Sun loves all the planets and can't pick just one. And all the meteors have left for a shower.

So that means that YOU will decide the favorite planet! That's right. You have studied the planets in school. You have read books and watched TV shows about them. Now it is time to pick YOUR favorite planet!

The winner is . . . who?

For Creative Minds

And the Winner is . . .

There are so many fun ways to incorporate math and science skills into learning about the solar system! Please see the free online teaching activities for more solar system fun.

Which planet do YOU think should be the Solar System's favorite planet? Why?
Ask your friends, family members, and classmates which is their favorite planet.

Copy or download this page from the internet (see above). Please do not write in the book!

Keep track of the answers using tally marks. For every answer, draw an "up and down" (vertical) line. Every 5th line should cross the four before it. Count the tally marks to see who the winner is and then graph the results.

Mercury	☿		
Venus	♀		
Earth	⊕		
Mars	♂		
Jupiter	♃		
Saturn	♄		
Uranus	♅		
Neptune	♆		
How many votes?		1-5	6-10

Mercury	Venus	Earth	Mars	Jupiter	Saturn	Uranus	Neptune

Planets are not to scale.

Time and Temperatures

Planet		Revolves around Sun*	Rotates on its axis*
Mercury	☿	88 days	59 days
Venus	♀	225 days	243 days
Earth	⊕	365.25 days	one day
Mars	♂	687 days	one day
Jupiter	♃	12 years	10 hours
Saturn	♄	29 years	10 1/2 hours
Uranus	♅	84 years	17 hours
Neptune	♆	165 years	16 hours

*The rounded lengths of time are shown in Earth time measurements.

Our day of 24 hours comes from the approximate amount of time it takes the Earth to rotate (spin) on its axis (a make-believe stick going through the Earth from the North to South Poles).

Our year (365 days) comes from the approximate amount of time it takes the Earth to revolve (orbit) around the Sun. We add a leap day every four years (leap year) to even out the extra fraction.

How long would a "year" be on other planets?

Do you notice a pattern between inner versus outer planets and the amount of time it takes them to rotate or revolve?

Find the planet symbol to identify the planet's average temperature.

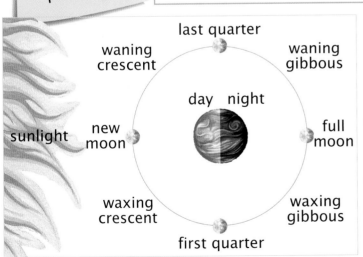

last quarter
waning crescent
waning gibbous
day   night
sunlight   new moon
full moon
waxing crescent
waxing gibbous
first quarter

How long would a "day" be on the other planets?

Our months come from the almost 30 days it takes the moon to revolve around the Earth. The first day of a lunar month is the day of the new moon, when the sun and moon rise at approximately the same time. The moon rises about 50 minutes later each day as it goes through its phases.

Food for thought: How long would a "month" be on a planet with no moon or with more than one moon? How would YOU determine how many months or how many days in a month? What would you call them?

Distance From Sun: A Place-Value Activity

Answer the following place-value questions. Answers are upside down at the bottom of the page. For more place value and decimal activities, see the book's online activities.

	Billions		Hundred Millions	Ten Millions	Millions	Hundred Thousands	Ten Thousands	Thousands		Hundreds	Tens	Ones
Earth			1	4	9	,	5	9	7	,	8	9	0
Jupiter			7	7	8	,	4	1	2	,	0	2	0
Mars			2	2	7	,	9	3	6	,	6	4	0
Mercury				5	7	,	9	0	9	,	1	7	5
Neptune	4	,	4	9	8	,	2	5	2	,	9	0	0
Saturn	1	,	4	2	6	,	7	2	5	,	4	0	0
Uranus	2	,	8	7	0	,	9	7	2	,	2	0	0
Venus			1	0	8	,	2	0	8	,	9	3	0

Planet distances are in kilometers.

1. Which planet's distance has the highest digit in the ten thousands' column?

2. Which planet's distance has the highest digit in the ten millions' column?

3. Which planet's distance has the highest digit in the hundred millions' column?

4. If you were to round to the millions, how far would it be in kilometers to Venus?

5. How many planets are over a billion kilometers from the sun? Which ones?

6. What place value do you need to look at to tell if Earth or Venus is farther from the Sun?

7. What is the value of the digit "5" in the distance between the Sun and Neptune?

Constellations, Famous People, and Space Technology

There are art references in this book to constellations, famous people, space technology, classic books, and even other art. Can you find the art in the book? What are some other things you see in the art? A detailed explanation of what is what and who is who can be found in the books' online activities.

Leo the Lion   Cassiopeia   Ptolemy   Copernicus   Mars Rover

Mariner   Cassini Space Probe

Hypatia   Galileo

Draco   Moon with Big & Little Dippers   The Herschels   Stonehenge

Place-Value Answers: 1, Earth; 2, Neptune; 3, Uranus; 4, 108,000,000; 5, three: Neptune, Saturn & Uranus; 6, ten millions place; 7, five ten thousands or fifty thousand;

Solar System True or False Questions

Use information found in the book to answer the following true/false questions. Answers are upside down at the bottom of the page.

1 Plants are at the bottom of our food webs and all life relies on plants for food. The outer planets have thick layers of soil for plants to grow.

2 Living things on Earth need liquid water to drink. All planets have water.

3 Living things on Earth need a safe, comfortable place to live. Temperatures on other planets would not support life as we know it—it would either be too hot or too cold.

4 Living things on Earth need oxygen. Many animals get oxygen through lungs and fish get it through gills. Since oxygen is also found on Mars, things that live on Earth might be able to live there too.

5 A day on Mars would be about the same length as a day on Earth but a day on Jupiter would only be 10 hours.

6 A day on Venus is longer than its year.

7 The inner planets are gaseous and have rings, but the outer planets are rocky.

8 We can only see the moon at night.

True/False Answers: 1. False: the outer planets are gas with no soil; 2. False: there may be water frozen on ice on some of the other planets (or on their moons), but scientists have not (yet) found liquid water on any planets; 3. True; 4. False: Mars' atmosphere has carbon dioxide, not oxygen; 5. True: a day is the amount of time it takes the planet to rotate on its axis; 6. True: a year is the amount of time it takes the planet to revolve around the Sun; 7. False: the inner planets are rocky and the outer planets are gaseous; 8. False: Depending on where the moon is in its cycle, we can see it during the day too.

Solar System Matching Activity

Can you identify the solar system objects? The answers are upside down on the bottom of the next page.

1   This planet is our home and is the only planet not named after a Greek or Roman god! Just over 70% of the planet's surface is water, and 97% of that is ocean or saltwater. Two percent is frozen ice or underground freshwater, leaving 1% freshwater from lakes and rivers.

2   It takes this satellite almost 30 days to revolve around the Earth, giving us our months. Depending on where it is in its revolution, we see it in different phases. We might see it during the day, at night, or not at all.

3   Named after the Roman goddess of love and beauty, this planet is too hot for life to survive. It has active volcanoes but no water or moon. It rotates (spins) in the opposite direction from all the other planets, and is about the same size as Earth.

Sun

Mercury   Venus   Earth   Mars   Jupiter

4   The largest planet was named after the Roman king of the gods. Astronomers believe the large red spot is a hurricane-like storm that has been there for over 100 years! This planet has different color bands from different gases, 62 known moons, and rings that are hardly visible.

5   The smallest of the outer planets and the farthest from the sun, this blue-colored planet was named for the Roman King of the sea. We know of 13 moons, the largest of which is called "Triton," named for the Greek god of the sea. Astronomers think that the dark spots are hurricane-like storms but much, much stronger.

6   This red-planet is often seen at night, without a telescope. The rover mission to study this planet brings a whole new meaning to "Red Rover." Scientists don't believe there is water on the planet now but think there was at one time. There is no oxygen on this planet but there is carbon dioxide in the atmosphere.

7   This is the star of our solar system, around which we revolve! It is a medium-sized star but looks so big because it is so much closer to us than any of the billions of other stars. It gives us the heat and light that we need to live. We see it rise in the east in the morning and set in the west in the evening.

Planets are shown in order from the sun and are scaled to size but not to distance. See the free, online teaching activities for a distance-from-the-sun activity.

Saturn   Uranus   Neptune

Library of Congress Cataloging-in-Publication Data

McGranaghan, John.
  Meet the planets / by John McGranaghan ; illustrated by Laurie Allen Klein.
      p. cm.
   ISBN 978-1-60718-123-1 (hardback) -- ISBN 978-1-60718-133-0 (pbk.) -- ISBN 978-1-60718-143-9 (English ebook) -- ISBN 978-1-60718-153-8 (Spanish ebook) 1. Planets--Juvenile literature. 2. Solar system--Juvenile literature. I. Klein, Laurie Allen, ill. II. Title.
   QB602.M34 2011
   523.4--dc22
                                    2010049632

Thanks to Dr. Curt Niebur,
Program Scientist, Planetary
Division, NASA; Dr. Susan
Niebur of Niebur Consulting;
Dr. Art Hammon, Program
Coordinator, CSU-NASA/JPL
Education Initiative, NASA/JPL
(Jet Propulsion Laboratory); and to
Brian Kruse, Lead Formal Educator at the
Astronomical Society of the Pacific for verifying the
accuracy of the information in this book.

Also available as eBooks featuring
auto-flip, auto-read, 3D-page-curling,
and selectable English and Spanish
text and audio

Interest level: 005-010
Grade level: K-5
ATOS™ Level: 4.3
Lexile Level: 760 Lexile Code: AD

Curriculum keywords: solar system,
anthropomorphic, compare/contrast,
data: do, measurements, place values,
rotation/revolution, scales/models,
technology, temperature

Manufactured in China, January, 2011
This product conforms to CPSIA 2008
First Printing

Sylvan Dell Publishing
612 Johnnie Dodds, Suite A2
Mt. Pleasant, SC 29464